The Sound
OF
Silent Songs

A BOOK OF POETRY

WAYNE TREBBIN, M.D.

To order additional copies of this book, contact:
Xlibris
844-714-8691
www.Xlibris.com
Orders@Xlibris.com

ISBN: 978-1-6641-9114-3 (sc)
ISBN: 978-1-6641-9115-0 (hc)
ISBN: 978-1-6641-9113-6 (e)

Library of Congress Control Number: 2021917200

Print information available on the last page.

Rev. date: 08/25/2021

Contents

Foreword

I enjoy writing poetry. It's hard work, but I enjoy it nonetheless. I believe poetry allows the reader to be touched in ways that pros rarely can. The imagery and rhythmicity and rhyming (when it is present), if properly applied, can bring forth emotions or stimulate thought often in a near visceral sense. One of the nice things about poetry is that the poet's input simply starts the process the reader will experience. The real value and truth of poetry is the reader's interpretation. What each individual reader gets from the poem is valid and real, and is an authentic interpretation even if it is not particularly what the author had in mind. Thoughts and emotions are personal and always authentic.

I have tried to craft my poems carefully. Some of them are, on the surface, a bit opaque and some are not. Some are serious or sad and some are light and some are outright frivolous. I have made sure that all of my poems have a musicality to them, and I would suggest that, in order to fully capture this, you read them aloud even if you just whisper them.

I have written this book and its predecessor, Moonlight and Quicksand, to stimulate interest in poetry. I think that over the last sixty years interest in poetry in America has declined. That is sad because it gives pleasure on so many levels. It is my sincere hope that readers of my work will experience the same degree of pleasure that I have found, all my life, in poetry.

Wayne Trebbin, M.D. May 30, 2021

Dealing With It

It's the mighty fist of time that circumstance shall wield,
And it's how we take that blow that makes us win or yield.
Time bites hard, and won't relent no matter how we try.
We are given what we have, and that's our full supply.
Gray will overtake a lifetime's other tones,
And aching robs the comfort of former stronger bones.
Yet real beauty's marked by kindness, and a willingness to share,
And we can find tranquility when things don't seem so fair.
So give to me a gentle mind and knowledge as my share
As I walk from younger days and tread where I would dare.

Living

The river's always moving; north to south it goes,
And we aboard our appointed rafts will stop where no one knows.
We go in one direction as we float the water's whim.
There's no way to defy it; we would drown were we to swim.
Some find the journey pleasant, reclining in the sun,
Others long for other routes that they would rather run.
But regardless of the preference, regardless of the goal
The river holds us captive 'til the freeing of the soul.

The Paradox

I looked sadly at the feathers on the ground.
There must have been a fight yet I'd heard not a sound.
The evidence was clear the bird fought to save its life,
But it's the way the world is, a place of mortal strife.
And yet the fox or other beast that brought about this scene
Had to kill to feed its young; it was nothing cruel or mean.
It's strange to think the finality brought about by death
Can foster life's vitality, and sustain our very breath.

The Jamboree

We have stuffed animals in our house. At night they come alive,
And dance around our bedroom, and happily they all thrive.
They run and jump and laugh a lot, and play their happy games.
I watch when they're not looking, and I've learned all their names.

Sometimes they'll have a party, and they'll sing their cheerful songs.
Other times they'll start to climb where none of them belongs.
It's very strange there's no one else who lies in bed awake,
For I would think it would be fun for others to partake.

There even is a grand march as they tramp throughout the house,
And the majorette's so tiny, a recruited little mouse,
But at five AM it's over, and they all come back to huddle.
Then they all do what they do best: return to us to cuddle.
This picture is from my camera

The Wolves

Wolves came into the moonlight, silent as they went.
It was the time of the hunt, and they were tracking a scent.
Their shadows glided smoothly as they came down from the hills,
And the only sound in the night was the cry of the whippoorwills.

There was nothing cruel about them; they needed to hunt to live,
And they would take from nature only that which nature would give.
Their hunger pushed relentlessly as part of the cycle of life.
And the herd they stalked oblivious to the approaching moment of strife.

There is a perpetual cycle of the predator and the prey,
And every living creature must fight within the fray.

Whispers Of The Sea

I feel connected as I stand here by the sea.
I can touch forever, and forever touches me.
With waves running in and out it breathes eternally,
And it is both immutable yet changing constantly.

When times are hard to handle like a mother it can be,
And with a gentle voice it resonates with me.
It's where life started, and it may save it in the end.
It delivers promises it will forever send.

Looking Back

There was a time when I was young
I looked to heroes not unsung.
And right was right and wrong was not.
It was a time I've not forgot.
There was a place I'll not return,
The path to which I can't discern.
I hear songs now unsung.
The world was sweet when I was young.

Keys

Be brave when times are really rough;
Be gracious when you can.
Be loyal to the ones you love;
Be quiet when you should.
It isn't easy to stay on course,
So focus through the glare.
Listen to the sounds of nature,
And respect the pure of heart.
It's always best to think things out,
But freely laugh on impulse.
Life always shares with us its beauty,
But it's up to us to look.

A Most Fatal State

I hope that I will thrive,
But fate I cannot change.
The world is full of choices,
And our struggles never end.

I've lived a life worth living,
Watched the long fight to survive.
There's something I have noted,
A condition none outlast.

No one can survive it;
It's a state that we all share.
That which I'm describing
Is to simply be alive.

Bobby's Mouse

Some people called him stupid; some people called him fool.
Bobby didn't fight back, but he knew that they were cruel.
No one ever talked to him. He cried a lot at night.
People told their stories, and laughed at him on sight.
Bobby shuffled into town, but no one did he greet,
And then he saw a little mouse standing at his feet.
He picked him up, gave a smile, something rarely done.
Soon they were companions, and Bob was having fun.
He told his mouse about his life and all about his pain.
He told of those who mocked him, those who were his bane.
The little mouse just listened, and never said a word,
But Bobby stood grateful for he knew the mouse had heard.
One day Bobby saw a cat; saw him jump and land.
He grabbed his little mouse then enfolded in his hand.
"I've got you safe my little friend." That's what Bobby said,
But when he opened up his hand his little friend was dead.
Bobby wailed in agony because his friend was lost.
He was so bereft he just couldn't bear the cost.
And then he looked again and laughed so very deep.
His mouse hadn't died at all, but had simply been asleep.

The Call Of The Whippoorwill

This is the sound
Of the whippoorwill,
Who sings his notes
On a summer's morn.
This is the sound,
And it's free and it's pure.
It softens my heart,
And widens my smile.

Author's note: These words were chosen as lyrics to the whippoorwill's song. If you say this poem out loud and accent the last syllable of each line you can hear the music of the bird's little tune.

The Maiden's Ghost

It was a night of dark foreboding, and there was no August moon.
The air hung wet and heavy, and the grass was wet with dew.
All around was silent save the sound of a single loon,
And I was more than full alert for the legend that I knew.

Two hundred years or more had passed since the maiden went to ground
When she went to meet her love on a summer night as now.
It was said he killed her, and her body never found,
But others said she left with him, but no one knew quite how.

The townsfolk went hunting him to make him pay for crimes.
They would have spurred their horses hard; so I doubt he could escape.
Some say her ghost haunts this field returned from other times;
That on a jet black mare she comes, bedecked in silk and crepe.

And in her soft melodious voice is the cold dead sound of fear.
They say the maiden both laughs and cries, with eyes that seem to glow.
I shift my cadence, increase my pace, for I don't want her near,
And why she lingers in this world I simply do not know.

I heard a horse approaching, hoof beats in the mist.
A summer breeze, a quickening freeze and then it passed me by.
Something brushed upon my cheek as if I had been kissed.
Then desperate I began to run. That's when I heard her cry.

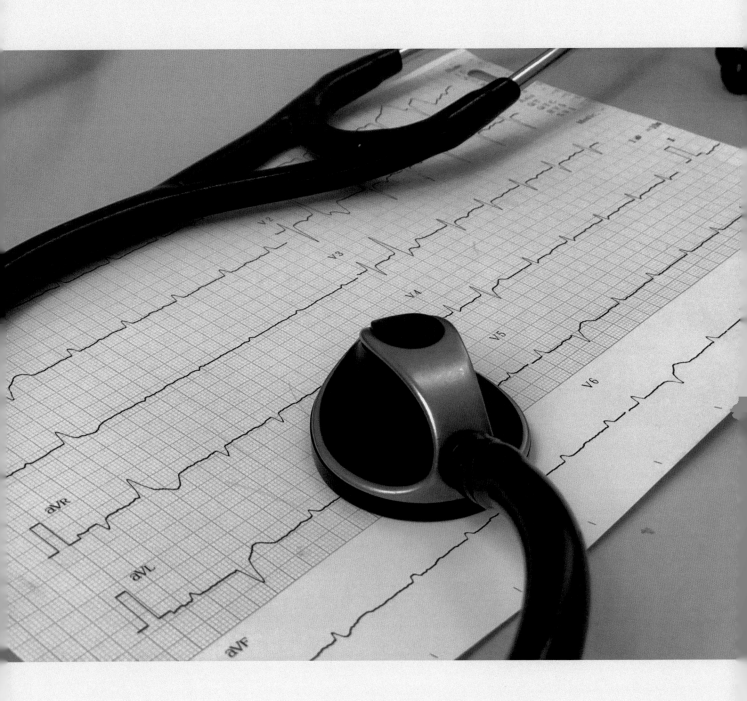

The Escort

She slept in fits, and he in the chair in her room,
And the monitor tapped out the ragged beat of her heart.
In the silence and dark was the looming presence of doom,
Yet long ago they'd promised never to part.

They had been happy together; through life they'd walked hand in hand.
He longed for her beautiful smile. He ached for just one more hug.
But now, at the end, their world was turning to sand.
The time had arrived. He felt eternity's tug.

He awoke, and there was a woman in black by her bed.
She glanced at him, a hood hiding her face.
She bent over the woman, but there were no words that were said,
And the monitor beeped a very irregular pace.

The end came that night with another sudden attack.
The hooded woman leaving him there in the dark.
None of the staff had seen this woman in black,
But she'd been the escort who helped the lady embark.

Misguided Fear

Something was moving around outside my house,
And I was not certain what plan was best to espouse.
Would it be wise to walk outside of my door?
Or might I encounter that which all would abhor.

I had no idea what was lurking about in the grass
Or if my strength and courage it would surpass.
Had evil come to hector me at the last,
Would it strike hard as it had through much of my past?

So I stayed up, worried and paced my room half the night
Not knowing what phantom that I was destined to fight.
Feeling the battle was lost and chagrined.
I opened my door…but all I found there was wind.

The Little Boys' Frog Pond

I have a friend I've known all my life.
When we were nine we had a great life.
One of our haunts was a watering hole
Deep in the woods, a little boy's soul.

It was a pond I don't know how deep,
And all about little frogs would leap
With big bulging eyes and big webbed feet.
We'd lounge, and we'd catch them in the mid-summer's heat.

A giant, granddaddy bullfrog lived there.
We'd been told, but didn't know where.
With sticks we prodded into the muck,
But try as we might we never had luck.

A mighty splash when our backs were turned,
Yet where that came from we never learned.
Had we caught him he'd come to know
We would have loved him, and then let him go.

Poor Judgement

The little bug went for a walk wearing his very best suit.
He looked in the mirror before he went out, and thought he looked very cute.
It was high noon, and the day was quite clear as he started across the lawn.
His would be a long journey, and he'd not return 'til next dawn.

He waved hello to the ants, who shouted "Hello Mr. Bug,"
And when he saw his favorite worm he bent over and gave him a hug.
He'd planned this trip for a very long time, and was happy to be on his way.
"All things considered," he thought to himself, "this will be a great day."

He heard a flutter from up in the air, and then something dropped from behind.
He turned, and saw a blue jay who said "What a wonderful find."
The bug began to ask what he'd meant then something happened so grim.
The bird simply opened his beak, and then he just swallowed him.

Changing the tempo there's a moral here,
I'll say it flatly and I hope you will hear.
The lesson is I'll say in a word
If you're a bug don't talk to a bird.

Rocky 1

When I first met him he was locked in a cage with a shadow over half of his face,
And you could tell by the way he stood that his trust was down to a trace.
Another person wrote a bad note, and the kitten had just been returned.
His life had been rough, and could turn on a whim as he had already learned.

I took him out of his cage, and looked him over with care.
I wanted to judge with compassion. More than that I hoped to be fair.
His fur was soft and not badly matted; his colors were white and gray.
The kitten lay still in my arms as I held him, attentive is what I would say.

And then with surprise I felt the vibration coming from deep in his throat.
Something told me this kitten was special, and I tossed back the previous note.
We took him home where he happily lives purring and playing and such.
He gave us his heart, and we gave him ours, and we happily love him so much.

Driving Through

The windows and the top were down,
And I gunned the car as I sped through town.
The wind and the sun were the summer's gift,
And the weight on my spirit had begun to lift.

I would avoid the bumps and slow roads.
I would avoid trucks with their loads.
There's nothing so great as a drive in the summer,
And I'll not opine how we'll all meet the drummer.

I wave to my friends, they smile at me.
There's joy in this ride, and that's plain to see.
The road in the heat is a shimmering thing,
And there are still songs that I'm yet to sing.

Some travel long roads, and some travel short.
It's all in the deeds that we all have to sort.
Some of us crash. And miles amass.
But one thing's for certain, in the end we all pass.

My Father

I have a picture of my dad when he was ten years old.
He's standing with a smile the whole world to enfold.
It's hard to see the man I knew within that smiling child,
The man with so much wisdom and a kindness oh so mild.

No matter what, he was steadfast, always on my side.
He taught me to tell the truth, to stand and never hide.
We'd go for walks, and we would talk, and he'd tell me all his tales,
He said be gracious when you win; be gracious when you fail.

He was such a guiding force, my hero to the end.
He taught me when to not give up. He taught me when to bend.
I stare at his boyhood picture, and wonder where he went.
He's now passed, but he'll be with me until my life is spent.

"The world is not just black and white, there's plenty of the gray."
There was so much he taught me. He had so much to say.
"Be calm in times of danger; kind and thoughtful as you go.
When you can, move quickly; but if you must, go slow"

There's a cycle to the universe for every living thing.
The older guide the younger, and sometimes angels sing.

A Snow Fall

The snow fall sets a muted stage as I walk through the wood,
And I would walk all this day in silence if I could.
It seems that nothing's moving save the falling of the snow,
And I enjoy the sense of peace in the forest that I know.
Sometimes there are track marks of harried squirrels and such,
And the air is pure and cold, and I just can't get too much.
It's days like this that give me joy, but days like this are rare.
I love the winter nexus between the snowfall and the air.

Letter To Carolyn: About My Journey

I've traveled long, and I've seen many things,
And in my heart our wedding bell rings.
I've seen poverty, sickness and dying.
And I've seen beauty that left me crying.
I've always tried to be someone good.
Sometimes I've failed and sometimes I could.
No one is perfect; it's just what we are.
I have worked hard at tracking my star,
And that star led me to your magic smile.
I love your sweetness and your elegant style.
You have such beauty born from your soul.
You hold my heart which you now control.
So with love I give you this little rhyme,
And with love I'll be with you 'til the end of all time.

The Frolic Of Words

Words leaped and jumped from my pen one day.
They were happy and glad to say
The words of poems about what I feel,
And they pulsed to a rhythm of that which is real.

These expressions danced on the paper.
And I was pleased to be the shaper
Of words that happily gave forth their song,
And that was a moment I'd wished to prolong.

Jamie

He makes us smile with his toothless grin of innocence,
And none can stand before his raucous laugh of joy.
There he sits ten toes gripped in both his fists
As he looks with pride at his happy new found skill.

When tenuous his eyes search out his mother and his father,
And his worries vanish to nothing in their arms.
In ten short months he's evolved in front of us,
And his future's still unwritten in the wondrous scrolls of life.

Will he be strong? Will he be tall? Will he speak with an orator's voice?
None of that's important. What matters in the end
Is will his life be enfolded in the love of those he loves?
For love will be the blanket that will warm him all his life.

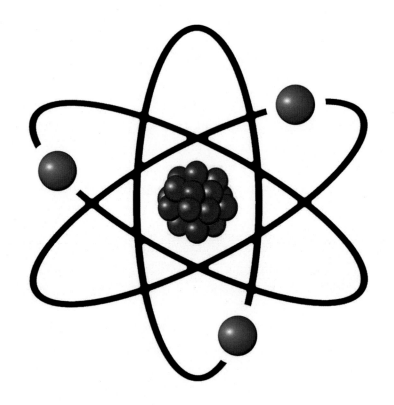

Rhythms I

The circle's a curious figure; it starts just where it ends.
In truth it's just a series of connected infinite bends.
It's always all around us, you only have to look.
There's something philosophical, a lesson that I took.

The moon rises silver, a lantern in the night,
And the sun her shining sister brings forth the morning light;
And our world spins on its axis as it travels round the sun.
Circles tucked in atoms with physics said and done.

Everything has its rhythms, and they truly bind us all.
Listen to the breathing tides and hear the universe call.

Coming Of Age

I almost drowned in the dessert heat;
There was nothing left for me to eat,
So I strapped myself into my seat,
And drove through the night myself to greet.

Then I looked for what was good,
And did the work I knew I could.
I struggled hard because I should.
It came with age that I understood.

I found a place I'd like to stay.
There's nothing absolute I'd say.
There's dues I fear that I must pay.
There is no black, there is no white.
The world itself is only gray.

Ode To Poetry

Poetry caresses the inner parts your mind.
It can make you run when you're just too tired to walk.
Poems can straightened your thinking when everything seems misaligned.
Verse can let you run like a deer and see through the eyes of a hawk.

I've been to the gardens of Babylon watching their rivers flow.
I've seen the prairies on Mars, and walked alone on the moon,
I can swoop like a bird so high, then dive so very low,
Yet if I close my book I sigh, returning to home all too soon.

Verse is my coupon, my own safe ticket to ride.
It stirs my feelings, and gently lends me perspective.
Life can be ragged yet we must try to abide,
And poetry shields us from life's intruding invective.

When I need to retreat to partake in a spiritual bath
I walk to my shelves, and pick up my favorite tome,
And then I find succor, and follow my personal path.
There is nothing so sweet and alive as a beautiful poem.

The Long Race

I hung on for the ride of my life.
Gave it my best, headed for strife.
It's a long way from home to never go back,
And sometimes it's courage I fear that I lack.

There are things that I would impart,
And I've watched as if blind right from the start.
No one completes the circle we race,
But we plow through exhaustion to keep up the pace.

And if you listen you might gain a tip.
Just never let go and don't dare to slip.
It's not the end but the process that counts,
And it's not always darkness that courage surmounts.

The 2020 Clash

Oh my country, my country, my home and my nation.
Where are you going, and what is your station?
We're in a maelstrom of turbulent times
Where the blind benighted dance out their mimes.

Darkly encroaching inveterate fools
Who threw away reason and stepped over rules.
We are one nation, and all need to know it.
When the anvil was struck a great flame was lit.

Johnny And Eva

The little boy and little girl together walked in stride.
One day they went for ice cream, and Johnny stepped outside.
Eva couldn't find him, and she began to cry.
He came back and saw her, and with a little sigh
He asked her what was wrong. She smiled as best she could.
She said, "I thought you left, and you said you never would."
Years later they were married on a lovely summer night.
Then his country called, and Johnny wished to fight,
But Eva whispered in his ear, "You promised not to leave me,"
And Johnny sat back in his chair, and he just let it be.
What they lacked in money they made up with their joy,
But Johnny wanted more for his wife and little boy.
A job was set with travel, and go he thought he should.
Eva said, "Please don't go. You said you never would."
Johnny held her, kissed her lips and then he dropped the job.
Years later Johnny caught a cough, and in the dark he'd sob,
For the doctor called it cancer, and Eva cried out, "No!
You promised not to leave me. Please, John. Please don't go."
But Johnny could say nothing. He knew the path he'd take.
He didn't want to do it, but this time his word he'd break.

Maintaining The Balance

Sometimes life betrays you;
Sometimes it hits you hard.
Yet sitting here at my window,
I still enjoy the view.

The sun begins to slip.
Its light makes gold the branches
That juxtaposed against the sky
Makes it worth the trip.

My story flows inside me
Like the blood within my veins.
I remember happy times,
And ponder what's to be.

The Elf

I am friends with a little elf who visits at the back of my house.
He's a tiny fellow who always rides in atop his favorite mouse.
We sit on the porch, and he tells me his tales of adventures, hard work and his wife.
He's traveled a lot, met fairies and trolls, and in general has had a great life.
One day as he brushed down his mouse he told me of exciting events.
There was a witch he met while out riding, and action began in moments.
She cast a spell, aimed for his head, and he ducked almost too late.
She wanted to eat him, but he would not have it, so she could not satiate.
Well he grabbed up the spell, and tossed it at her, and she disappeared into smoke.
He explained that witches can't stand the sight of good solid elfin folk.
I pointed out that's really not fair to judge with prejudice blind.
And he told me we all need to think there's justice our world needs to find.
In the issues of elves and the issues of people there is a lot we can share.
He made the point we have much in common and each for the other should care.

Froggy

Froggy's a friend I've known since age four.
Together we chased pirates and thieves.
We had adventures, and always sought more.
We lived in a world only children perceive

He was of rubber, a tough little guy.
He wore a red coat and big floppy shoes.
I'd take him to play, and I swear we could fly.
We would fight evil, and we'd never lose.

Now I'm a grown man, and he's an old frog,
And I still have him; he lives in my drawer.
I know if I took him he'd still be agog.
Because fantasy comes when you open its door.

Pansies

I love little pansies with their happy little faces.
I have them all about my house in a multitude of places.
It's as if they look at me with stories to be told.
Red, yellow, orange, blue just lovely to behold.

In the summer heat they greet me my charming little friends.
They always make me happy as a gift an angel sends.
I care for them with soil, and I water them each day.
I want to share their magic so this poem's what I say.

Rocky 2

Rocky is a cute young cat, white with big gray patches,
And through the house he'll sprint hard with the devil on his tail.
He loves his little mice of cloth, and plays with what he catches.
And if you leave food around he'll steal it without fail.

When he purrs and nestles me I always find my smile.
Sometimes we laugh when he hides. His tail gives us a clue.
I love it when he lies with me and sleeps a little while.
He'll push things off the counter, but there's more he's apt to do.

The thing that's most important and what's for us the best
Is that we really love him, that mischievous little pest.

Stop Point

I simply can't believe it; they found me dead at home,
And here am I not moving as I lay in state.
Done are my adventures. Still I wish to roam.
And I cannot accept it. I can't believe my fate.

I was once a child, laughing with my friends,
In my teens I explored the mysteries of my youth.
There are lessons I have learned that only living lends.
And as a man in the fray I looked to find the truth.

Was I a good man or a simple greedy fool?
Did I stand for kindness or was I closed and cold?
I certainly knew anger, but I hope I wasn't cruel.
I clung to my standards so my honor I would hold.

Tomorrow I move on. I go into the ground.
Will it be to Heaven or will it be to Hell?
One thing is for certain, I'll not make a sound.
I won't hear them talking nor listen to the bell.

Walking in the mist of what there is to be,
And I will be from this world totally set free.

Integrity: The Portal And The Ogre

The portal was an ancient thing for millennia in the wood.
And before the bridge that crossed the river a hiking couple stood.
The bridge was old and sagging, and didn't look too sound.
But they tried to cross, and it was the portal that they found.

When they reached the other side the world began to turn,
And they would begin an adventure as they were about to learn.
There could be great danger, and possible rewards.
They would have enemies with whom they might cross swords.

She now wore a flowing gown like none she'd ever seen,
And somehow he now wore a doublet made of velvet green.
In her hand she held a dirk, and a sword was at his side.
They were, of course, both confused, and there was no place to hide.

Before them ran a little path which they chose to take,
And they would not veer right nor left just for safety's sake.
A sudden sound made them stop and hold their breath as well.
It was the sound of fury. It was a sound from hell.

Suddenly as if by magic there an ogre stood.
He was huge and muscled. He would hurt them if he could.
In one hand he held a sword, in the other a silver shield.
"I am the king of ogres," he roared, "and it's power that I wield."

Now all around him minions stood, eager for a fight,
And the man and the woman stood back to back keeping all in sight.
"You will become an ogre or you can choose to die."
But the man spoke with defiance, "just step over here and try."

"We are fated human. We'll not change what we are."
The ogre sneered, then he said, "Start praying to your star."
The man and woman then broke loose, and ran to where they started,
And with the knife and sword they hacked until the stay lines parted.

The bridge plunged down to the water, and its parts were swept away.
The portal was gone; two worlds now separate; and the ogre had been held at bay.
Sometimes principle holds things together, and what matters can stay the same.
So history's written, and we can determine: do we take the name or the game.

A Good Day's Sail

The air was crystal with clear morning sun.
The ocean was vast, and we were for fun.
Cutting through water, enjoying the sound,
And we in the boat were glory bound.

The boat heeled to starboard so we sat to port,
Lines neatly coiled with nothing to sort.
Crisp dry air filled our lungs and our souls,
And off the bow there came gentle rolls.

From days like this are great poems born.
No trace of worry on this early morn.

Cleo Cat

Her head tucked in, curled up tight, Cleo lay on our bed.
Our sweet black cat, small, refined; happy she'd just been fed.
When I stroke her little face she purrs, and shuts her yellow eyes,
And while she's smaller than her peers her face just looks so wise.

She came to us bedraggled, pregnant, scrawny and all alone.
We gave her milk, and we watched her drink all just skin and bone.
Something had broken her tail in the past, and it just hadn't healed quite right.
We let her in to our home and our hearts; she was such a pitiful sight.

For one full year she stayed upstairs afraid to leave her place,
And then one day we looked around; through the kitchen we saw her race.
Now self-assured with confidence she roams about the house,
Yet wouldn't you think after all we've done she could at least catch us a mouse.

Sometimes You Just Have To Flee

The squirrel, running its heart out, jumped over a hillock and tried to break free.
It knew it was hunted, but lost in a field it just couldn't find a tree.
Eons of desperate instincts poured forth, in an effort to keep it alive,
And it was not certain terror and speed today would help it survive.
A blast of a shotgun fractured the air, and the little guy dodged to the right.
A second shot missed its mark. He jumped and went out of sight.
The hunter stood silent, scanning the field, hoping to get one more shot,
But the squirrel had put distance 'tween him and the boy, and dying would not be its lot.

My Mother

My mother lived to ninety five.
It's life itself you don't survive.
Bent and deaf and nearly blind;
Thankful she still had her mind.

She was a beauty in her time.
That loss was aging's subtle crime.
My father loved her 'til he died,
And she loved him, and so she cried.

Not much is sung of stoic steel.
As we are pulled by livings reel.
It was her courage saved her smile,
And it was grace that marked her style.

A Summer Night Remembered

Like full moon light in the purple night
Spilling over and out of sight.
One might think it even right
To stand at the edge of time.

In the silvered splash where I would go
I cross fields, and I walk slow,
But there is something I would know
For the summer night's a charm.

Is this real or so I think?
Does history greet me with a wink?
From the bowl of life I would drink.
Mortality runs ahead.

Rhythms II

Like the giant glow of a prairie fire
Or the changing light of a funeral pyre.
The western sky orange and red,
With darker clouds by angels led.

The day was darkening as night approached
Attacking the light it now encroached.
Warmth withdrew a slow retreat.
Yet in twelve hours the two would meet.

It is the rhythm of our world
Like sails let loose and then refurled.
I love the stillness of the hour.
It's time itself that has the power.

The Car Accident

A car flipped over at the side of the road,
A little boy down on the grass.
The father's guilt his personal goad.
There was no way we could pass.

The rear window where the boy shot through,
A circumscribed hole where he struck.
To drive on by just wouldn't do.
The boy seemed just out of luck.

He didn't move when I knelt at his side.
I felt sinking despair.
I was surely convinced he had died.
Sometimes it just isn't fair.

Odd though it was there was no blood,
And then he opened an eye.
And I could feel my emotions flood,
And I felt that God was nearby.

I believe that miracles happen.
This was an amazing day.
Sometimes the ropes of fate can slacken,
And the boy just walked away.

Author's note: This is a true story. It occurred when I and my medical team were doing medical missionary work in Latin America. The boy had shot through the car's rear window head first with an impact that seemed for all the world one that no one could have survived, yet he was completely unscathed.

The Visitor

"Mama am I dying?" the small girl softly spoke.
"No my dear that's not true," her mother's voice now broke.
"Mama I don't feel good," as she slowly closed her eyes,
And her mother prayed for all the time that chemo often buys.

Suddenly the child stirred, her eyes now open wide.
"Look there at the window the one that's by your side."
Her mother noted nothing there, just an empty chair.
She turned toward her daughter, and gently stroked her hair.

"There's nothing there my darling. Try to sleep," she softly sighed.
The girl said "Grampa's sitting there." It was two years since he died.
The mother stiffened visibly her face went drawn and pale.
"No Dad, please don't take her, just let your mission fail."

She could not see him as she spoke, but she knew her daughter could.
She knew what his mission was, his purpose understood.
She pleaded that he leave them, and let her daughter stay.
And then she cried as her daughter said, "Mama he went away."

The Dragon Fighter

I once fought a dragon with just a sword and shield.
He was really very big, and just refused to yield.
We fought all day and through the night 'til we could barely move,
And other dragon fighters came, and they would all approve.
The dragon roared, and I would duck as he breathed his fire at me,
And at last he gave up, but then I set him free.
It's amazing what is written in the archives of brave men,
And I will always smile remembering when I was ten.

Break Out

The screaming spirits of the night
Were pounding on my door,
And though locked out and out of sight
They clearly wanted more.

They were born inside my brain,
And then they came to life.
I felt that I might go insane
Their anger was so rife.

Moonlight splashed across my floor,
But shadows flickered through it.
This was a page from ancient lore,
Yet I would not submit.

I thrashed about in agitation
For they were now inside.
I prayed this was imagination
I could not simply hide.

Sometimes real is not so real
Sometimes the issue's tough.
Was I bound my fate to seal?
I had had enough.

Sometimes what we fear so much
Is nothing that is real,
But keep the monsters out of touch
So as not to seal the deal.

The Studio

Life is like a sculptor's tool that cuts and shapes the clay,
But the changes come on slowly, a little day by day;
And so the flesh gets thinner, and wrinkles find a place.
Strength's replaced by other things, and hollows mark the face.

All of this has import, but it's not the sculptor's goal,
For when the clay is riven it's the revealing of the soul
That determines if it's art we have or a simple waste of mud.
It's a study of the best of us; the kindness and the blood.

On Politics

Sometimes the engine stalls,
And the wheels refuse to turn.
That's when the gliding eagle calls,
And the rubber starts to burn.

I've watched this forever.
It's duty holds me tight.
Sometimes I think that I will sever,
And truly end the fight.

So it's virtue in the offing,
But that can change with time,
And I can't seem to stop the scoffing,
Of those who missed their prime.

The fight goes on forever,
And no one wins the game.
I struggle in my own endeavor,
But all remains the same.

Pixies

I know a place where the pixies all go.
It's in the field where the sycamores grow.
There's running and laughing and plenty of singing,
And somewhere among them are tiny bells ringing.

The wee folk are happy, a likeable lot,
But if you're not quiet, you'll see them not.
Sometimes they're tricky, they'll borrow your things.
Then they'll run away quickly, as if they had wings.

When I lay in the moonlight behind an old tree
I'm always delighted by something I see.
For example tonight a wedding there was
By a little wee preacher for that's what he does.

And oh what a cry of joy from the crowd.
Two pixies united, and the cheering was loud.
All through the banquet they chattered away,
And throughout the night I decided to stay.

If you wish to visit my pixie friends
Stay in the shadows where the moonlight ends.
Don't make a sound or you'll scare them away,
And remember good pixies sleep all through the day.

Cracked Ice

When I was twelve we lived near a lake.
One winter my mind I seemed to forsake.
I tromped on the ice, and after a while
Something occurred that got me to smile.
There was a loud noise like slamming a door,
And I thought that was fun so I wanted some more.
Then I jumped up and down pounding the ice.
I wanted more cracks… thought that would be nice.
In general I can say as a group
Little boys give meaning to the word nincompoop.

Yin And Yang

The storm was fierce, and trees were felled,
The rain was strong for one full hour.
What seemed so harsh had goodness held
Born witness by a purple flower

Art

Last night I saw a wondrous sunset
One that I will not forget.
The sky just came alive.

From west to east the sky was flushed
With clouds of gold with silver brushed
Royal grandeur all.

It entranced and I was caught,
My brain enveloped with one thought
This art's the work of God.

The Cricket's Message

There was a cricket singing just outside my door,
And when he stopped his tune I still hoped for more.
He's music song of nature, simple, sweet and pure,
And in the search for wisdom of this I'm very sure.
Most struggle is for nothing, yet we keep the pace.
It's often not important that we continue in the race.
The cricket doesn't worry, he just sings his little tune,
Happy in the sunlight on this lovely day in June.

Ghosts On The Beach

The first wave came in with a crash, and then sucked back to the sea.
The next was bigger with a plume of spume, and it too ran back to the sea.
The third wave, a giant, came in with a roar, and hit with a rattling thud.
This was a show of power, of nature hammering free.

The rain obscured his vision, like a faucet ran off his face,
And the waves continued their pounding, and all ran back to the sea.
No craft would be safe on that ocean; no skipper calm in that storm
For the wind and the tides and the devil, all took part in this case.

Delilah had gone for a sail that day when the sky had been clear and bright.
He had told her weather was coming, but she only laughed and set out.
There were warnings the storm would be big, but she had missed all the cues.
Now heart beating fast he stood by the sea, and she was nowhere in sight.

They were to wed tomorrow after this mid summer's gale.
She was his love and he was her life, and forever they hoped to be
Walking together the ribbon of fate hand in hand to the end.
He focused his gaze, but the storm blocked his way; he could find neither hull nor her sail.

Still the waves pounded the beach then returned to their matron the ocean.
He whispered her name over and over as if he were speaking in prayer,
And all around the storm lashed out beating its rhythmic tattoo.
He felt the world out of control, all was confusion and motion.

Delilah's boat never came home, and consumed by grief was he.
She would never return to him. She was forever gone.
Yet he refused to lose her. He would defy their fate.
And so he sailed out to meet her. Then both were embraced by the sea.

Some times when summer storms arrive with people who watch and who wait
A man and a woman are seen by the shore laughing in spite of the rain.
Clearly in love, enjoying each other they frolic about in the storm.
Hand in hand forever together, walking their ribbon of fate

On Brutality

The stag, the horses and men, were running a frightening pace.
Dashing along in a field of grass, and death was the prize of this race.
The stag bounding off for the sheltering woods dashing with beauty and grace;
The horses spurred on, eyes open wide, and madness touching each face.
The men held their guns, and one took a shot.
He'd hoped he had hit but he'd not.
The stag turned left then he dodged to the right;
Kicking up clots of turf as he ran, keeping the forest in sight.
It was not panicked but focused, running with smooth liquid speed,
And none of the hunters could match him no matter how fast were their steeds,
Then one man stopped, took steady aim, and calmly fired his gun,
And the stag went down, kicked once or twice; the race now over and done.
There was no remorse in the man, just gratified over his kill,
And the stag just lay in the grass, eyes wide open and still.

The Struggle

Words spoken softly in the dark
Rose one day to strike a spark,
And there was a time the cause seemed lost,
But we fought on despite the cost.

Had we quit would villains be,
But we pressed on so all could see.
Yet destiny is not secure;
Still there are things of which I'm sure:

All humankind is family,
And I swear I'll die free.
No one is better than another.
I call them "Sister." I call them "Brother."

I don't know when the fight will end.
Perhaps the wounds will someday mend.
There are few of better good
Than those who strive for brotherhood.

Printed in the United States
by Baker & Taylor Publisher Services